Sunflower Happiness

By
Jacqueline Morton

Time with God inspired through prophetic drawings

Written and Illustrated: Jacqueline Morton

Printed by Ingram Spark Australia.

Acknowledgements:
Scripture quotations from the Holy Bible New International Version Anglicised
Copyright 1997, 1984, 2011 by Biblica.
Hodder and Stoughton Publishers, as Hachette UK company All rights reserved.

First printing, 2022.
ISBN: 978-0-6453763-0-2

Published by Jacqueline Morton
Adelaide, Australia

Publication assistance by Immortalise

Hanging out with God

Contents

Introduction

My name is Jacqui and through my paintings within I hope you find a stronger sense of peace, hope, guidance and comfort.

Sunflowers make me smile! I mentioned this to my dad one day while going through a particularly hard time in my life. Three days later a member of my church, unknown to me, came to my workplace and gave me sunflowers as they felt strongly that God wanted them to do so. It was incredible! God wanted me to know I am loved and for me to find peace and happiness in everyday life.
It was this moment that inspired me to share with you all - Love, Peace, Joy, Happiness and Hope and to know that you are so dearly loved.

My artwork started as a mindfulness activity and I found profound messages and words coming to mind during and after creating them. Messages through words of hope, peace, joy, guidance, encouragement and love. This is how God was communicating with me. These are my art works and the messages associated with them.

(The reflection points are to help prompt further thinking and time with God to delve deeper into your relationship with Him and yourself. Read the words but you can also let God speak through the drawings.)

The Bigger Picture

Step back and realise there is a beautiful bigger picture right in front of us.

Colossians 3:1-2
"Since, then, you have been raised with Christ, set your hearts on things above, where Christ is, seated at the right hand of God. Set your minds on things above, not on earthly things".

If you focus on one twig in the forest you can't see the view.

Sometimes we get so focused on a goal, problem, work or a task, that we lose sight of a bigger plan and the bigger picture of life.

It's easy to do and I am also guilty of this.

- If something is troubling you I implore you to look at the bigger picture of your life. Your problem is valid and may need attention, however, taking a step back can give us perspective.
- Give your problem to God and allow him to work in that space.

Blossoming under God's care

Galatians 5:1

"It is for freedom that Christ has set us free. Stand firm, then, and do not let yourselves be burdened again by a yoke of slavery".

Surrendering control to God is freedom.

When we are covered and surrounded by God in our everyday lives we find there is less stress and worry because we trust that it's in God's hands. We can relax and swim (easier said than done sometimes).

When I remember that God has my life in his hands I can let go and let God takeover. Through life with Jesus we grow and blossom in God's Love, guidance and transformation.

- What worry or concern can you give over to God to take care of?
- How can you see God's transformation in your life?
- How can you share this freedom with others?

Doing life with Jesus

John 8:12

"Then Jesus again spoke to them, saying, "I am the Light of the world; he who follows me will not walk in the darkness, but will have the Light of life".

The boat looks peaceful, calm and a beautiful place to take in the spring weather. To get there we can swim and get wet or go with Jesus and walk there with a friend. When I start trying to do life on my own and nothing seems to be working I need to remind myself I'm not alone, I can ask for help, and I can do life with a friend, in the big and little tasks in life.

- What is an area of your life you can invite Jesus to walk with you in to find peace?
- How will it be different with Jesus? If you're not sure why not ask him to walk with you and find out.

Transformation

Romans 8:14-17

"For those who are led by the Spirit of God are the children of God. The Spirit you received does not make you slaves, so that you live in fear again; rather, the Spirit you received brought about your adoption to sonship. And by him we cry, "Abba, Father." The Spirit himself testifies with our spirit that we are God's children. Now if we are children, then we are heirs—heirs of God and co-heirs with Christ, if indeed we share in his sufferings in order that we may also share in his glory".

Butterflies represent new life, we are new in Jesus but life is about transformation and we are being constantly shaped into Jesus' image.

Butterflies struggle in the cocoon in the transformation process, just as we struggle in life. God says he is working for our good in everything we go through and it will be okay because we are his sons and daughters.

- Who are you? Whose are you?

Boxes

What do you put in boxes?

If we packed up our lives into boxes, we have labels such as spiritual, personal development, work and career, health and fitness, relationships, finances, hobbies and recreation.

They are all separate but intertwine

- How does God intertwine into the boxes of your life?
- Is he in all areas of your life?
- Where in your life currently can you acknowledge God more?

Peace and Purity

Psalm 23:2

"He makes me lie down in green pastures, he leads me beside quiet waters".

We all experience peace in different ways and situations. When I finished and looked at this drawing I felt an overwhelming wave of peace roll over me. And have every time since.

At this time in my life God knew I needed peace and found a way to give it to me.

• Where or what is your place of peace? What does it look, smell, sound or taste like? Is God there? Could he be?
• How do you experience the peace of God in your life?
• Lay with God and ask for what you need today. Not sure what you need? He knows... let him give it to you.

Tangled

Over time our life takes many twists and turns. Our lives bear fruit in times of celebration, success, enjoyment but life also, as we all know, has hard times that can hurt and although we move on they are still a part of our life.

The decisions we make teach us many lessons. No one is perfect and it is the actions and choices of our past (the spikes life gets tangled in) that are our reminders to not make the same hurtful decisions twice… three or four times.

Thank God for hindsight and learning from past decisions. In hindsight we can see God's involvement in our lives.

There are certain parts of our past we may not like or may feel ashamed of. We need to ask for forgiveness and then receive it. That's right, receive it! Accept our past decisions and move forward with Christ moulding us by his side.

There are no mistakes but lessons to be learnt with opportunities to grow.

John 9:25 He replied: "Whether he is a sinner or not, I don't know. One thing I know. I was blind but now I see."

- When you look back through your life- How do you see God at work?
- Is there something you're holding onto because you're embarrassed, ashamed or worried about? I encourage you to give that to God and allow his forgiveness to saturate your being. Let him work in you.

Laugh Kookaburra Laugh

Life can be so serious! Laugh often and Love much.

Create fun, exciting and silly moments where you can laugh with each other, at each other and yourself.

Ecclesiastes 8:15
"So I recommend the enjoyment of life, for there is nothing better on earth for a person to do except eat, drink and enjoy life. So joy will accompany him in his toil during the days of his life which God gives him on earth".

This is not to say just sit around eating, drinking and nothing else, but to do these things and enjoy the work you do knowing with gladness in your heart this is the day the Lord has made, rejoice and be glad in it. This is where you shine as a Christian and make others question... what have they got that I don't?

• How can you create some fun and enjoyment in your week?

e.g. - Intentionally play a board game with someone, go out and see some friends, play with your children/ grandchildren, sit and enjoy a quiet moment and soak in the calm and peace of the moment... Whatever it looks like for you - do it intentionally as this is the day the Lord has made for YOU!

Rise from the Ashes

Romans 8:17-18
"Now if we are children, then we are heirs—heirs of God and co-heirs with Christ, if indeed we share in his sufferings in order that we may also share in his glory. I consider that our present sufferings are not worth comparing with the glory that will be revealed in us".

Do you ever feel at a loss in situations, don't know where to go, a little helpless? There are many bible verses to encourage us when we are in a situation like this and can't see a way out or forward, whether it's for ourselves or a friend.

Philippians 4:13 "You WILL rise from the ashes of your situation"!

This doesn't always give immediate relief and comfort to all, however, over time you will heal stronger and more brave than you were before. Have some of these verses with you wherever you go, or a photo of this image as a reminder that with Gods help you will rise.
Joshua 1:9, Isaiah 41:13, Matthew 6:34, Psalm 121:1-2, James 1:2-4 , Psalm 46:1, Romans 8:28

- Do you connect better with an image or the word?
- Which of these verses resonates with you? Carry it with you on paper for a couple days and read it when you feel you need it. Or an image that gives you hope, strength and confidence.

Bee families

1 Corinthians 12:12

"Our bodies have many parts, but the many parts make up only one body when they are all put together, so it is with the "body" of Christ".

A bee is an amazing creature. Their hive depends on the pollen collected by workers who risk their lives collecting it. Within the hive is an intricate network of different tasks to be done to ensure survival and they all protect their queen. Their queen has two purposes- to help regulate unity between the colony and to lay lots of eggs.

Our world isn't so different. This drawing inspires the way I see God is looking for us to live. Living in unity with one another, working together to serve each other and ultimately to serve and love our King.

We cannot do life on our own and were never created to.

We are all individual with unique gifts to work together. Is something calling you to work in a certain area? Be involved in certain projects? Do you have a passion for something in particular? Maybe it's God calling you to enjoy and use your gifts to bless others and in turn yourself.

• What might be calling you?
Ask God to reveal your passions and current direction.

Running Strawberries

Interesting fact- Strawberries grow runners. Strawberry runners are horizontal stems that run above the ground. Each runner has a tiny plant at its end and these can be rooted and grown on to produce new plants.

As we learn about and share life with God we come across opportunities to share with others. Share what you have learnt by communicating bible stories as well as our own testaments about how we see God working in our lives. God was not just working during biblical times but is working in our hearts and minds now. Sharing our encounters as well as bible stories to excited listeners. Who doesn't love a great story!
Sharing your life and opportunities with people continues the runners. Running to share the fruit with others could be making a huge difference in their lives.

Romans 10:14-15
"How, then, can they call on the one they have not believed in? And how can they believe in the one of whom they have not heard? And how can they hear without someone preaching to them? And how can anyone preach unless they are sent? As it is written: 'How beautiful are the feet of those who bring good news"!

- Have you felt called to share with people around you?
- Would you be ready to share with someone?
- Who is one person this week you could talk to about how God is working in your life? Christian or non-Christian.

Discovering Presents

James 1:17
"Every good and perfect gift is from above, coming down from the Father of the heavenly lights, who does not change like shifting shadows".

It is easy to focus on all the things we are lacking, things others have and we don't, things we've missed out on. With this kind of thinking we can easily pull away from God and try and do life on our own assuming we need to do it ourselves because God has not given us all the things we want.

With effort we can flip this way of thinking and with persistence, encouragement and assistance we can live in a world where we lack nothing and have so many amazing gifts from God in our lives.

Gifts come in many forms- physical, spiritual, environmental, people, places, emotions, your body….

- Make a list of all the good, amazing and wonderful things, people, experiences you have in your life.
- You could add to this daily. A daily gratitude journal thanking God and realising the incredible gifts you keep receiving.

Aren't you excited to see what he has to give you tomorrow??

Slow and steady

Jeremiah 17:7-8

"But blessed is the one who trusts in the LORD, whose confidence is in him. They will be like a tree planted by the water that sends out its roots by the stream. It does not fear when heat comes; its leaves are always green. It has no worries in a year of drought and never fails to bear fruit."

Our relationship with God and ourselves isn't a sprint, it's a marathon. When we invest time and effort into a relationship, whether that be with a friend, work colleague, our children, partner, family, with ourselves or with God, we learn and grow together along the way creating roots that run deep. When our worlds are shaken these deep roots help hold us steady.

- When life gets tough what or who do you rely on? This is where your roots are.
- Is there a relationship that needs work in your life? So when your life or the life of those you love is shaken your roots will hold you both strong?

When we have a strong relationship with God we are strengthened in life's ups and downs, work on your relationship with him and he will take care of the rest.

- Set aside a time this week to commit some time, it may be only a few minutes, to God and your relationship that needs attention.

Passion Rose

Bold, bright and passionate. These are the words that come to me as I look at this picture.

A rose symbolises love.

Love can be seen to be at its strongest and most bold, bright and passionate when we are in times of darkness.

When a child is scared, when one lives in fear and are supported by the safety of their loved ones, when one is in a season of deep love, grieving or struggling with something they see the true bold and passionate love of friends and family.

God is holding you and surrounding you with this passionate, bold and bright love always and can generally be seen in all its glory when darkness is near. God is light. Where there is light darkness cannot be.

John 1:5 "The light shines in the darkness, and the darkness has not overcome it".

- What are 5 things you love about your life?

Find the light in the darkness for all good things come from Heaven.

Scarlet

Scar - Let

Let the scar be there

We all have scars - deep ones, superficial ones and hidden ones (Physical or metaphorical).

Jesus had scars too. When he returned he wasn't ashamed of them, they were a representation of where he came from and where he was now. They told an important story. With the scars you are perfect.

Loving ourselves with all the scars of the past can be hard when we see them as ugly and immoral but they are why you are where you are today. Jesus kept his scars. They proved he was victorious; you can be too!

Luke 24:39 "Look at my hands and my feet. It is I, myself!"

- Where were you in life days, weeks, months, years ago?

Ride the wave

Light at the end of the tunnel

Jude 20-21 "But you, dear friends, by building yourselves up in your most holy faith and praying in the Holy Spirit, keep yourselves in God's love as you wait for the mercy of our Lord Jesus Christ to bring you to eternal life".

A golden heaven in the distance where the wave is headed, the wave of life we ride Darkness and blockages get in the way as we ride the wave there. When we lose sight of Jesus our boards get wobbly, however, when we remember and trust he is there he will steady our board and calm our minds. Even if we are unsteady at times in life, this strengthens our legs and balance in life to be able to pick ourselves up and move forward, and have the courage to take on anything coming our way with Jesus' support.

When we lose sight and try to ride the wave on our own, we can ride too high and we end up bobbing in the ocean, having to paddle the whole way on our own strength. If we go too low on the wave we end up on the beach stuck and walking, carrying our heavy board. Therefore, when we go off the path focusing on distractions from our purpose in Jesus we end up exhausted. Trying to walk or paddle the whole way on our own… we won't make it there on our own strength.

- Are you paddling or walking in your own strength at the moment? Are you trying so hard at something that just isn't working? Do you need to push your board back into the wave and stand back up with Jesus? Give him the problem and watch as he guides you back up on the board and through the wave. His wave will guide you all the way, as you continue to strengthen and balance.

- When life gets wobbly or if it is currently wobbly how will you put your trust in him to strengthen you and steady your board to get you to your destination?

Turn to face the Son

Young sunflowers turn from east to west during the day to follow the sun to increase growth and stay warm.

When we as humans are in the sunlight our bodies get Vitamin D, this allows us to stay strong in our physical body. It helps our immune system to modulate cell growth which helps our emotional body by increasing serotonin - A hormone that increases our mood. What a beautiful worldly comparison and reminder of how we can turn to the 'Son' to promote our growth and strength in faith and relationship.

1 Chronicles 16:11 "Look to the Lord and his strength; seek his face always".

Storms in life are coming and going, big and small, short and long. The Son is a steady light. When we turn to him consistently we learn, grow and strengthen to withstand the strongest winds.

Storms will try to shake us but as it says in Philippians 4:6
"Do not be anxious about anything, but in every situation, by prayer and petition, with thanksgiving, present your requests to God".

 • How do we turn to Jesus? Read the word, pray, talk with other Christians, read a daily devotion, continuously hand over your worries and praises to Jesus.
 • What is one thing this week you will do to seek Jesus more?

www.ingramcontent.com/pod-product-compliance
Lightning Source LLC
Chambersburg PA
CBHW041053050726
47599CB00018B/2130